Media Literacy for Kids

Learning About Primary Sources

by Nikki Bruno Clapper

Consultant: JoAnne DeLurey Reed
Librarian and Teacher

raintree

a Capstone company — publishers for children

Raintree is an imprint of Capstone Global Library Limited, a company incorporated in England and Wales having its registered office at 7 Pilgrim Street, London, EC4V 6LB – Registered company number: 6695582

www.raintree.co.uk
myorders@raintree.co.uk

Edited by Gillia Olson
Designed by Cynthia Della-Rovere
Media Research by Wanda Winch
Production by Laura Manthe

Photo Credits
Anne S. K. Brown Military Collection, Brown University Library, 13; Bridgeman Images: Leemage/Private Collection, 21; Capstone Studio: Karon Dubke, 17, 19; CriaImages.com: Jay Robert Nash Collection, 22 (bottom); Dreamstime: Spotmatik, 9; NASA: Johnson Space Center, 5; The Richmond-Times Dispatch, cover (Titanic newspaper article); National Archives and Records Administration: David M. Rubenstein Gallery, 11; Newscom: ABACA/PAPhotos/Whyld Lewis, 15, akg-images/Marion Kalter, 22 (top), Photoshot/UPPA, 7; Shutterstock: Action Sports Photography, cover (bottom left), David Smart, cover (top right), Donna Beeler, cover (soldier), LiliGraphie, cover (br), mtkang, cover (frame bl)

ISBN 978-1-4747-0429-8

Printed in China

Contents

Like a time machine

What was it like to walk on the Moon

for the first time?

This photograph can give you an idea.

It is a primary source.

US astronaut Buzz Aldrin
walking on the Moon in 1969

A primary source helps you to find out about the past. It comes from someone who was part of history. A primary source is an original, not a copy.

These are pages from the diary of Anne Frank. She and her family were in hiding from the Nazis during World War II.

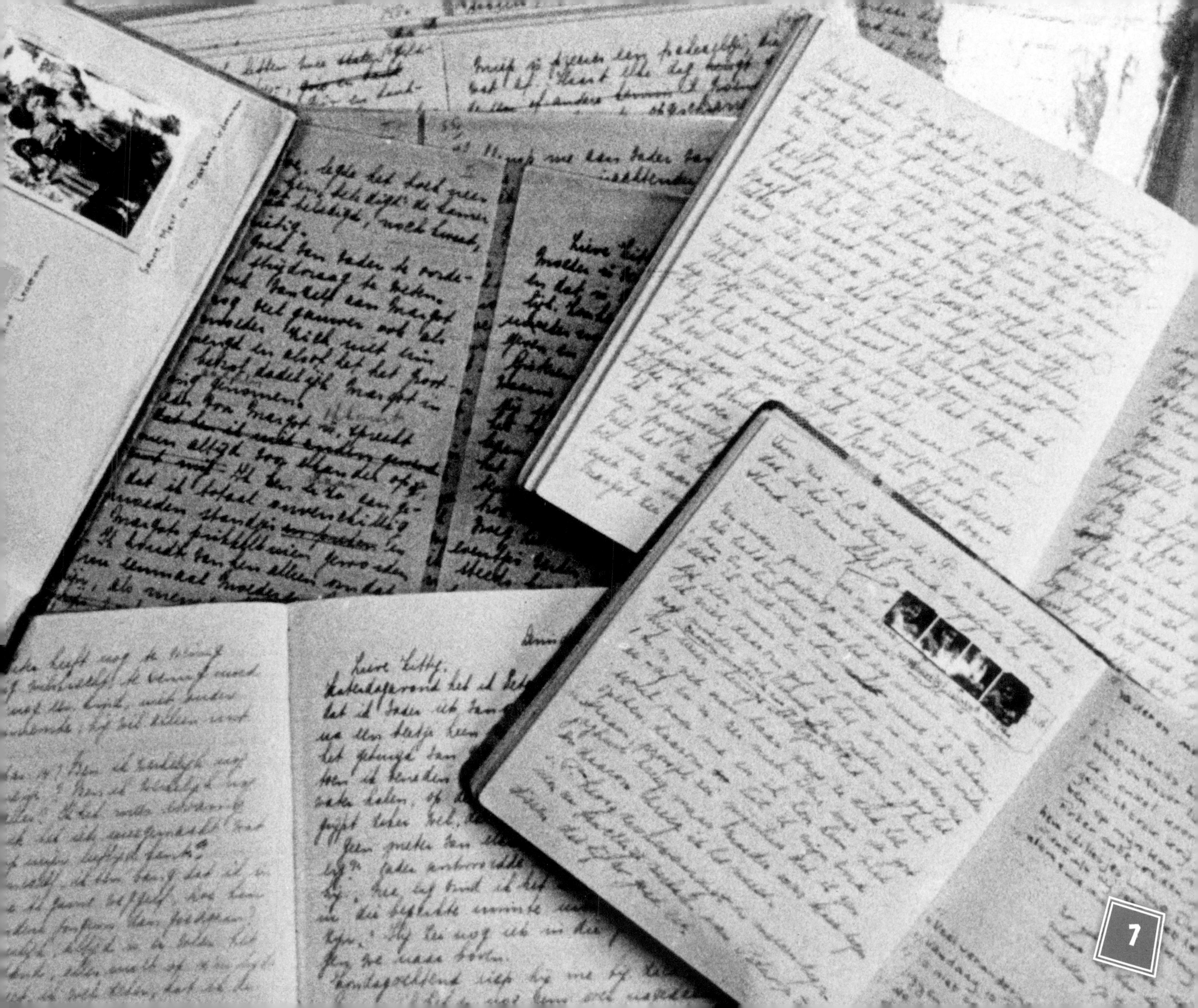

7

A primary source can be a letter, a photo, a painting or a diary. Anybody can create a primary source. Your family photos are primary sources.

Families look at photos to see their own history.

Three primary sources

This primary source is a document, or piece of writing. It is called the Magna Carta. It was signed in 1215, and is the basis for our laws.

The Magna Carta was signed by King John.

This primary source is a painting. It is a portrait of Benedict Arnold. He became famous as a traitor in the American War of Independence.

This portrait was painted in 1776 by English painter Thomas Hart.

A primary source can also be an object, such as a coin or a piece of clothing. Objects can show us how people lived in the past.

Queen Elizabeth II wore this dress for her coronation in 1953.

Primary or secondary?

People use primary sources to create secondary sources. Some examples of secondary sources are non-fiction books, articles and encyclopedias.

Libraries are full of books that are secondary sources.

Authors of secondary sources
describe a time in history
they did not see. They may
write about what happened
50 years ago.

This woman is reading about a time
before she was born.

If you really want to feel like a part of history, find a primary source. Go back to the moment. Then look, listen and learn!

An archaeologist examines the remains of King Tut, who lived more than 3,000 years ago.

Activity: Primary sources and your senses

Primary sources help us to experience history through our five senses. We can hear sounds on a video. We can see an artist's creation in a painting. We can smell or taste food by following an old recipe. We can feel emotions by reading a diary or touching the tools of a famous inventor.

An instrument played by Mozart, a famous composer in the 1700s.

An 1887 advertisement for land in the American Midwest.

1. Look at the two primary sources on this page.

2. For each primary source, write the answers to these questions:

   What type of primary source is this? (A document? An object? A photo?)

   Which senses does the primary source help you to use? Why?

Northern Kansas.

AN INVITATION

IS HEREBY EXTENDED TO EVERYBODY DESIRING
A CHOICE HOME IN THE

FINEST COUNTRY

IN THE WORLD,

TO VISIT THE PLACES

DESCRIBED IN THIS FOLDER.

Glossary

archaeologist person who studies human history by digging up remains and objects

author person who creates a work of art

composer writer of a piece of music

document piece of paper that contains important information

encyclopedia book or website that gives information on subjects that are usually arranged in alphabetical order

original something new and unusual; the first version of a work of art

primary source work of art made by someone who is part of history; primary sources can be documents, photos, videos, or objects

secondary source an account of an event from someone who did not experience it firsthand

Read more

Christopher Columbus and Neil Armstrong (Comparing People from the Past), Nick Hunter (Raintree, 2015)

Education Through the Years (History in Living Memory), Clare Lewis (Raintree, 2015)

Websites

www.bbc.co.uk/schools/primaryhistory/british_history/magna_carta/

Find out more about King John and the Magna Carta.

www.britishmuseum.org/explore/young_explorers/create/chocolate_puffs.aspx

Follow this old recipe and taste some treats from Georgian times!

Comprehension questions

1. How are primary and secondary sources different?

2. Look at the photos in this book. Which primary source would help you to study something that interests you?

Index